MORE BOOKS FROM THE SAGER GROUP

The Swamp: Deceit and Corruption in the CIA
An Elizabeth Petrov Thriller (Book 1)
by Jeff Grant

Chains of Nobility: Brotherhood of the Mamluks (Book 1-3)
by Brad Graft

Meeting Mozart:
A Novel Drawn from the Secret Diaries of Lorenzo Da Ponte
by Howard Jay Smith

Death Came Swiftly:
A Novel About the Tay Bridge Disaster of 1879
by Bill Abrams

A Boy and His Dog in Hell: And Other Stories
by Mike Sager

The Deadliest Man Alive: Count Dante, The Mob
and the War for American Martial Arts
by Benji Feldheim

Lifeboat No. 8: Surviving the Titanic
by Elizabeth Kaye

The Pope of Pot:
And Other True Stories of Marijuana and Related High Jinks
by Mike Sager

See our entire library at TheSagerGroup.net

GOING HOME TO DIE NO MORE

A TRUE KENTUCKY STORY

RUSS WITCHER

Published in the United States of America.

Cover and Interior Designed by Siori Kitajima, PatternBased.com
Cover: (Left to right) William P. King, Abraham Owens and Wesley Finn, circa 1867.

Cataloging-in-Publication data for this book is available from the Library of Congress
ISBN-13:
eBook: 978-1-958861-05-9
Paperback: 978-1-958861-06-6

Published by The Sager Group LLC
(TheSagerGroup.net)

GOING HOME TO DIE NO MORE

A TRUE KENTUCKY STORY ABOUT A TRAIN ROBBERY AND A HANGING AFTER THE CIVIL WAR

RUSS WITCHER

THE SAGER GROUP

Artifex Te Adiuva

To Jackson Yates Witcher,
the best part of my history

ACKNOWLEDGMENTS

I would first like to thank James H. Snider, president of the Simpson County Historical Society in Franklin, Kentucky, for supplying me with documents that were invaluable to my research in the King-Owens murder case. He also took me on a tour of the jail where Captain King and Private Owens were incarcerated during their trial with the other men who faced the jury's verdict. Judge Bill Harris of Franklin also kindly shared with me his private research he had done on the King-Owens case.

The Logan County Kentucky Archives in Russellville, Kentucky, provided me with court records pertaining to the derailment and train robbery charges that helped to complete this story.

Mike Sager of The Sager Group has always been generous with his time and support, not only to me but to the students in my Literary Journalism class.

My wife, Tera, has been great to accompany me on any research endeavors, whether it be to take a detour on our honeymoon to go to the Richard M. Nixon Library and Birthplace to do research for my dissertation or to go to cramped jail cells and take photos of graves in old cemeteries as she did for this book. That is indeed work above and beyond the call of duty.

Stories do not write themselves, but after this book, I do believe there are stories that want to be written. I'm glad I got to be the one to write this story.

"Going Home to Die No More"

My heavenly home is bright and fair;
Nor pain nor death can enter there;
Its glittering towers the sun outshine;
That heavenly mansion shall be mine.

Chorus

I'm going home to Christ above,
I'm going home to the Christian's rest,
I'm going home, to die no more,
I'm going home to die no more.

My Father's house is built on high,
Far, far above the starry sky;
When from this earthly prison free,
That heavenly mansion mine shall be.

(Chorus)

Let others seek a home below,
Which flames devour or waves overflow;
Be mine a happier lot to own
A heavenly mansion near the throne.

(Chorus)

—Lyrics, William Hunter, 1838

"I am told that of the number of books there will be no end; all purporting to be the life and history of Capt. P. King, the great railroad robber and murderer, etc. Now this is all stuff and a means used as a deception in order to make money. My life, adventures, dreams, secrets, and comments on the trial and testimony are all in the hands of a careful and, I trust, faithful compositor, which will not be published until I shall have been done with the troubles of this my earthly hell. Though I be a 'murderer,' as the world is wont to call me, I feel there is a better day coming; and if the just vengeance of heaven ever overtakes my enemies, they will suffer much.

"But in this I take no pleasure, for I can forgive my most violent enemy; and if need be, could embrace him."

— Excerpt of a letter Captain William P. King wrote from prison to the Louisville *Journal* for publication on June 27, 1867, the day before his execution on the gallows in Franklin, Kentucky.

CONTENTS

INTRODUCTION

My great-grandfather, James Lafayette Witcher, lived to be ninety-three and was a Union veteran of the Civil War, serving with Company F, 52nd Kentucky Infantry from November 1863 until being honorably discharged as a private at Bowling Green, Kentucky, in January 1865 at the age of twenty.

My father was seventeen when his grandfather died in 1938, so he knew him well. He said his grandfather didn't talk much about any skirmishes he fought in during the war, but he did talk about living off the land by robbing smoke houses when they were hungry and taking clothes off clothes lines when they needed something to wear. He also said Cordell Hull on occasion spent the night at his house when he was riding as a circuit judge in the early 1900s between the courthouses in Lafayette and Celina, Tennessee, a distance of some forty miles.

I had not gone beyond this family folklore until I looked up the roster of Company F, Kentucky Infantry, USA, and found that his captain, William P. King, had been hanged in 1867 in Franklin, Kentucky, for having murdered King's brother after their involvement in a train robbery. Captain King, along with a private from King's hometown of Franklin, Abraham Owens, had been hanged for murdering the brother after he told of their involvement in the robbery.

King and Owens and a party of ten other men had robbed a Louisville & Nashville Railroad train in November 1866. King and Owens murdered King's brother, Harvey, when they suspected he would turn state's evidence against them for the reward money L&N was offering for information leading to the capture of the robbers.

King and Owens were subsequently convicted of murder, and after the governor delayed their execution twice and King and Owens failed to escape jail twice, they were executed in Franklin in June 1867.

Although King and Owens had lived in Franklin since the 1850s, they had been born in Macon County, Tennessee, as had my great-grandfather. I later discovered during my research that my great-grandfather's honorable discharge had been signed by Captain King.

GOING HOME

On Thursday, November 8, 1866, a little after 2 a.m., engineer Jim Stewart was piloting his Louisville & Nashville locomotive five miles north of Franklin, Kentucky, on its way to Nashville. He spotted crossties and rails placed on the train tracks before he applied the brakes and put the engine into reverse. The momentum of the locomotive caused it and the express car behind it to jump the track and turn over twice down a forty-foot embankment. The front of the locomotive was now pointing back toward Louisville. The baggage car and the smoking car were behind the express car and were also derailed but only partway down the embankment. Behind the smoking car were the ladies' car and the sleeping car, which remained upon the track.

There were approximately one hundred passengers aboard, including women and children. Ten to twelve men with revolvers, their faces blackened, fired a volley of shots into the air. The robbers boarded the wreckage and proceeded to take money and watches from the passengers in the cars that were still on the tracks. Then, the express car behind the locomotive started to burn because a stove on board had overturned in the crash. The robbers ran to the bottom of the embankment, but the fire had already consumed the money safe and packages that were aboard.

The fire then raced up the embankment and overtook the baggage car and the smoking car. The baggage master and mail agent had thrown baggage and mail bags from the burning car, and some of the robbers took light baggage with them as they made their getaway about thirty minutes after the derailment.

Other than a few cuts and bruises, the only people aboard to be significantly hurt were the engineer, who hurt his leg and was unable to walk, and the express agent, who was severely bruised by falling boxes in the express car.

The conductor of the train, Charles Rice, walked the five miles into Franklin after the robbery and returned with a locomotive around 4 a.m. from Mike Lipman's circus, which was on its way to perform in Nashville. This locomotive was attached to the ladies car and the sleeping car still remaining on the track and took on board the passengers, baggage and mail and made it into Nashville around noon.

The L&N Railroad estimated the damage to its new locomotive at $10,000 and the three burned cars at $3,000. The railroad estimated the loss to the Adams Express Company of the money and packages in the express car to be at least $10,000. The Louisville *Courier* reported that $25,000 burned in the express car.

Captain S. B. Brown from Louisville had his carpetbag taken, which contained $10,000 in vouchers. About an hour after the robbers had left the scene, Brown followed their trail and found his valise two miles from the railroad. It had been cut open, his clothes taken but the vouchers left as if they had no value.

The passengers were able to hide some money from the robbers, for they were able to make up a monetary gift as well as a signed testimonial to engineer James Stewart:

> We, the undersigned, passengers on the night train from Louisville to Nashville on the L. and N. R. R., which was thrown from the track by a party of armed outlaws for the purpose of plunder, do hereby tender our most sincere and heartfelt thanks to Jas. Stewart, engineer of engine No. 1, who at great risk to himself did most nobly stand to his post even after the engine had been thrown from the track and turned over two complete turns down an embankment of forty feet—thereby saving life and limb to many of us. Had he jumped from the train as soon as he had somewhat checked its speed, which he might have easily have done, and which self-preservation most certainly dictated, the entire train would have inevitably been precipitated down

the embankment and serious loss of life would have been the result. We do, hereby, pronounce him a brave and noble man.

***

The L&N Railroad wasted no time in seeking to catch the robbers. The company had one of its pay trains robbed just the previous month north of Bowling Green, Kentucky. Suspicion focused immediately on Confederate guerrillas still tormenting the borderland. Ellis Harper, for instance, had been responsible for approximately 20 deaths in this region during this period. In fact, the Louisville *Courier* reported that a passenger on the train that was robbed north of Franklin said to one of the robbers that he had been a Confederate soldier for four years. To which the robber replied, "Young man, this is no political affair." Still, the *Nashville Daily Press and Times* continued to see the plunder in such terms in an editorial published the week of the robbery:

> The people of Sumner and other counties who harbor and pet (Ellis) Harper and his followers as if they were a set of heroes and a band of brothers instead of treating them as a pack of graceless scamps are, in a great measure, responsible for such robberies as that of Wednesday night. They claim, nevertheless, that they are loyal and law abiding. Now is the time for them to show their faith by their works. They will entitle themselves to the gratitude of the community to say nothing of an approving conscience if they will now set bravely to work to rid the country of a gang of worthless fellows whose defiance of the laws and whose frequent outrages are a damning blot to the fair fame of Tennessee and Kentucky.

Ellis Harper's outrages included Harvey Travelstead and the family of Hensley Harris. Travelstead, who lived in Simpson County, of which Franklin was the county seat, was killed by Harper after he learned Travelstead had disclosed his movements to federal authorities during the Civil War. Harper went to Travelstead's church while he was attending services, dragged him out and shot him. Hensley Harris, another Simpson County resident, was also suspected of giving information of Harper's whereabouts to federal authorities. Harper and his men went to Harris's home and demanded that he open his door. When Harris refused, Harper's men shot into the house, killing Harris's three-year-old son. With the war over, in May 1865, Harper was paroled by the federal command in Gallatin, Tennessee, but the governors of both Kentucky and Tennessee still had warrants for his arrest. The Commonwealth of Kentucky pardoned him eventually, and in July 1868, Tennessee Governor William Brownlow rescinded that state's warrant.

A reward of $2,000 had been offered by the Louisville & Nashville Railroad for the capture of the robbers of the pay train that took place in October just north of Bowling Green, Kentucky, but that had been unsuccessful in leading to an arrest.

Albert Fink, general superintendent of the railroad line, now offered a reward of up to $10,000 for the arrest and conviction of all of the robbers of the passenger and mail train north of Franklin, Kentucky, the following month. Even a partial reward was offered:

"There were from ten to twelve men engaged in the robbery. If all cannot be arrested, one thousand dollars will be paid for each one that is arrested and convicted."

In his 1867 book, *Railroad Robbers or the Life of King and Owens*, John J. Ditto Jr. wrote that the first robber to be arrested in Franklin was Abner Owens, who was sent by train on November 13 to prison in Louisville. The next day, seven additional men were arrested for robbery in Franklin and taken by train to Louisville: Wesley Finn, William Finn, Abraham Owens, Joseph Payne, Charles Smith, David Wainscott, and Stephen Cornwell. Of the seven arrested that day, Cornwell, described to be about twenty years of age, made a full confession. Cornwell also identified Captain William P. King from Franklin, who had not been arrested, as the ringleader. Once at Louisville, Cornwell was placed in jail, while the other six men arrested were confined separately at Taylor Barracks, the military prison there. On Thursday night, King was arrested in Franklin and taken by train to prison in Louisville, the ninth person to be captured in the party. King told authorities there that his brother, Harvey, had been involved in the robbery and had told him who else was involved in the robbery and that his brother was subsequently killed for telling this information. King said the killer was Abraham Owens.

The *Chicago Tribune* reported in its November 17 edition that Robert Hoy, a Negro, and John Colbert, a mulatto, were also brought up to Louisville by train from Franklin on Friday night and held by the military. Finally, the Louisville *Courier* reported on November 19 that the last suspect, John Evans, was captured in a cave near Franklin and taken by train to the Louisville prison on Saturday night. Like Stephen Cornwell, Evans made a full confession of his guilt.

The description of Evans by the Louisville *Courier* is too good not to set down:

The prisoner is a farmer and has been a resident of Simpson county for a number of years but was not a soldier on either side during the war. He is represented to be an indolent, worthless fellow, who has never accomplished anything beyond a meagre support for his wife and several children. He is the owner of a pack of hounds and has devoted much of his time to fox hunting.

In appearance, he is the most villainous of all the captured desperadoes, his ugly countenance seemingly reflecting the baser thoughts of a depraved mind and classing him with those in whose vile company he has been wont to mingle. He is over six feet in height, with long, bushy, dark-brown hair and clothed in a suit of seedy blue jeans as dirty and filthy as their uncouth wearer.

While on his way to this city, he relieved the monotony of a railroad ride by frequent draughts from a Pike's Peak bottle, which he kept in his pocket as a sort of talisman that might serve to ward impending danger.

The dozen prisoners were originally taken to federal prison in Louisville because of obstructing and robbing the mail, according to Ditto's book, but they were never charged with this crime and were returned to Franklin to await the decision in December of the county grand jury.

The thirteenth member of the robbery party who never made it on the train to Louisville—Harvey King, the younger brother of Captain King—had been shot three times by someone after having told about his knowledge of the previous week's train robbery. The robbery party had taken an oath before the robbery that anyone who told about the robbery would be killed. Abraham Owens asked to borrow a revolver from Captain King the Saturday before Harvey King was murdered.

According to Ditto's book, on the Sunday morning that Harvey King was killed, Captain King left his mother-in-law's home where he and his wife lived to look after a field of corn that some cattle had gotten into. While on the way to the corn field, he met his brother, Harvey, who was leaving their mother's home where Harvey lived. King asked Harvey to help him fix the fence where the cattle got in, but Harvey replied that he had forgotten something at home and turned back. King said Harvey then passed over a little hill, and he heard someone speak to Harvey in a familiar voice saying, "How are you, old fellow?" After that, King didn't see Harvey again. He drove the cattle out of the field and went to his molasses factory but did not see Harvey the rest of that day. He said he then went to the house of William Owens Sr. to tell him to keep his cattle out of his cornfield. Owens wasn't there, so he told Abner Owens about the cattle. Still not finding his brother, he concluded that Harvey was drunk somewhere.

Later that Sunday morning, King was getting wood and met Abraham Owens and John Prather. Owens told King, "I will return your pistol tomorrow morning by my small brother." King said, "All right," and the two men rode on.

The pistol was returned to King as agreed upon on Monday morning while King was at work in his molasses factory. A young boy who worked at the factory took the pistol to King's mother's house that morning. Later Monday morning, King and his sisters who worked with him at the molasses factory noticed turkey buzzards flying overhead. King rode in the direction of where the buzzards were flying and found Harvey's body with three bullet holes in it and his head severely beaten.

King didn't testify at the murder trial, but he did testify under oath at an inquest at his mother's house over the body of Harvey King held by Dr. Ventrees. During the inquest, King was asked to identify the voice he heard speaking to Harvey King on Sunday morning. King said he didn't recognize it but afterward said it was the voice of Abraham Owens. He said he didn't testify to this at the time because William Owens Sr., Abraham Owens's father, was on the coroner's jury.

King also testified to the coroner's jury that on the Tuesday after Harvey's body was discovered the previous day, he and a neighbor, Griff Wright, had gone to King's mother's house and taken the pistol he had loaned to Abraham Owens. It was only then that King discovered there was blood on the pistol and that it had been sprung in the stock as if it had been used to hit someone.

The grand jury indicted all twelve members of the party for the murder of Harvey King and for the previous week's robbery and derailment of the passenger train. Because the December session of the Simpson County Circuit Court was set to expire, Judge George C. Rogers called for an extra session of the circuit court in January 1867 to hear testimony in the murder case of Harvey King. Stephen Cornwell and John Evans were dropped as defendants because of turning state's evidence in the murder case. It was determined that the robbery and derailment case would be heard at the conclusion of the murder trial. No bail was allowed for the ten defendants.

***

The attorneys for the prosecution were Judge William V. Loving of Bowling Green; William Thompson of Russellville; and Charles W. Milliken, John A. Finn, and William W. Bush, all of Franklin. Attorneys for the defense were George W. Whiteside of Franklin and Walter Underwood, B. C. Grider, W. W. Western, and H. H. Skiles, all of Bowling Green.

Judge Rogers called the extra session of the circuit court to order on Monday, January 7, and ordered Sheriff Ira J. Bogan to set about to empanel a jury.

More than twenty witnesses for the prosecution began testimony on Tuesday, January 8, starting with Evans and Cornwell, who had turned state's evidence. The prosecution finished presenting witnesses on Thursday, January 10, at which time the defense began with a series of more than thirty-five witnesses that wouldn't conclude until the following Monday, January 14.

Evans testified that the robbers got about $11 each, including some clothing, pocket knives, and valises. Evans testified that Harvey King was at the train robbery and took the oath to kill anyone who told about the robbery. Evans further testified that Captain King told him after the robbery that Riley Towe, a resident of Franklin, had told King the name of every man involved in the robbery. Evans testified his conversation with King took place the Saturday evening before Harvey King was killed. During this conversation, Evans testified that King offered Evans $10 to kill Towe and that Towe was in sight of Evans and King while this proposition was being made to him.

Both Evans and Cornwell testified that William Finn and David Wainscott held the horses during the robbery. Cornwell further testified that King, Abraham Owens, Abner Owens, and Wesley Finn entered the passenger train and demanded money.

The aforementioned Riley Towe was another person put on the witness stand for the prosecution. Towe testified that King talked to him about joining in the train robbery, saying to Towe that he believed they could make $1,000, and if they were caught, they could "pay out." Towe testified that after the robbery he saw Harvey King the day before Harvey was killed on Sunday and asked Harvey who the large man was on the train when it was robbed. Harvey replied that it was Wesley Finn. Towe said Harvey told him who all the robbers were. Towe told King the Saturday evening before Harvey was killed what Harvey had told him about the robbery, and King replied, "Tut, tut, tut." At that point in their conversation, Towe said King told him there was a jar of money about twenty-five miles away and King wanted Towe to go with him to get the money that a young man that he had confidence in had told him about. Towe further testified that he later saw King and Evans talking together that same night.

Towe said that the Monday he found out Harvey King was killed, he was walking up to where Harvey's dead body was lying and where other people had gathered, and Captain King caught him by the sleeve and took him aside and sat down with him on a log. King told Towe to say nothing about what Harvey King had told him. Towe told King that was the reason Harvey was killed, and King told him not to talk so loudly.

Towe said that after the robbery, he told his son John, who had worked at the Kings' molasses factory for twenty-five days, to watch out for the Kings. John had been sent home to stay all night for the first time since his employment on the night of the robbery. Riley Towe had possession of a knife that his son had discovered that Harvey was distressed about having lost. Riley gave the knife to Dr. Thompson, who showed the knife at the trial. Towe said he believed this discovery "put the ball in motion" to convict the robbers, and he thought he had as good a right as anyone to collect the reward money the railroad was offering for their conviction.

It should be noted at this point, the Louisville & Nashville Railroad only offered money for the conviction of robbery, not murder. In fact, no murder had been committed when the reward offer was posted.

Dr. Ventrees testified next. He was the coroner of Simpson County and had held an inquest over the body of Harvey King. He said King was shot three times, but it was his opinion that only the ball that went through Harvey King's breast was large enough to fit the pistol exhibited on trial. The other wounds under King's arm were too small to have come from a ball that would fit the pistol exhibited. Dr. Ventrees was put back on the stand by the prosecution the next day and testified that after he thought about it and consulted with authorities, he now thought that wounds under King's arm might appear smaller because Harvey King had his arm elevated when he was shot.

John Towe testified that after the robbery, both Captain and Harvey King had said at the molasses factory that they were scared of guerrillas because they heard the train had been robbed by Confederate guerrillas.

Captain King had tried to send five letters from prison in Louisville back home to Franklin via a fellow prisoner who was being released named William Griffin. Griffin gave these letters to the prosecution for submission at trial. The first one was addressed to his brother-in-law, W. M. Reeder, who lived with Reeder's mother as did Captain King and his new wife, Ellen:

> I am under arrest for the train business. You know that I am not guilty. See if Mary & Louisa was not at our house that night and your mother and you and them all state that I was at home that night. . . but you all stand up. I will come out all right. They have nothing against me only what that Steve Cornwell has told he has stated that I was along. I don't know when I will get away from here. I want all the help I can get. See if the girls & your mother will. I want to make as strong proof as possible.
>
> My Dear Wife: I would like to be with you. Put confidence in no one. I am not allowed to write what I want to.

He wrote a second letter to his wife, Ellen, saying essentially the same thing.

A third letter was addressed to everyone in the household:

"If you will all swear for me, I am clear. All agree upon one thing and go to lawyer Bush and have a statement that I was at home all night and I can get bail then when court comes off, I will get clear, and if you don't, I am gone up. You know I am clear."

Lawyer Bush, from Franklin, would actually be part of the prosecution team.

The fourth letter was addressed to his mother-in-law, which read in part:

"Ms. Reeder you are the oldest. You know how to fix everything. Ellen was sick. . . and we all set up with her until 2 o'clock & Mary

& Louisa was there. You see them and tell them they have to swear that."

The last letter was addressed to his wife's family:

"You and your mother & Mary & Louisa, Ellen was sick that night and we set up until after 2 o'clock. This has to be done and I am clear. Now you all have to do this. Don't let any one see this. Don't tell old Griff Wright anything. I send this out by a friend."

James Smith, who lived in the neighborhood with both King and Owens, also testified for the prosecution. Smith said he was on the coroner's jury and King had testified as a witness there and said he had seen his brother Harvey about 7 a.m. on the Sunday that Harvey was killed. King said he had loaned his pistol to Abraham Owens on the previous Saturday evening, and he was to return it to him on Sunday, but it was not returned until Monday morning. Smith said the pistol King showed him was bloody and that King thought the pistol had been used to kill his brother. King said he did not believe the pistol had been shot but did believe that Harvey had been struck with it. Smith testified that King later told him that Abraham Owens' younger brother Billy brought the pistol to him on Monday morning as Billy was going to school. King said he hadn't examined the pistol until Tuesday when he noticed the pistol had been sprung in the stock. It was not in that condition when he loaned it to Abraham Owens.

A neighbor of King's named William Welty, who lived about four hundred yards from where Harvey King's body was found, testified he had heard three gun or pistol shots in "quick succession" about 9 o'clock the Sunday morning Harvey King was killed. He said the sound of gunfire came from the direction of where Harvey King's body was eventually found. Welty testified that King had come to his house about 11 a.m. that day and had asked if Harvey was there. Welty told him he was not, and King left.

Another neighbor, John W. Hendrick, testified that he also had heard three shots in "rapid succession" at about 9 a.m. that Sunday.

J. W. Thompson testified that he was on the train the night it was robbed. Thompson said that he had recognized Wesley Finn on the train and Abner Owens's voice. He said he had worked for Owens and knew his voice. Thompson further testified that on the Monday after the train was robbed that he had ridden with Owens for a short distance, and Abner had asked him if he knew anyone who was on the train. Thompson replied that he didn't and said Owens replied to him he would be killed if he did. Thompson testified that Owens had said there were "one hundred men standing ready to shoot him" if he told anything. Thompson said W. E. Waldron was also on the train that night, and he had told Waldron not to say anything either because Waldron had recognized Owens on the train.

Waldron was next on the witness stand and said he had recognized Owens on the train. He'd previously worked with him for about twenty days. Waldron testified he had told Thompson that Owens was one of the robbers, and Thompson had replied for him to be quiet or he would be killed. Waldron testified that Owens had come to see him at the oil well where he was working on the day before Owens was arrested and had asked Waldron if he knew anyone who was on the train the night it was robbed. Waldron had told him he was "so damned scared" that he didn't want to know anybody. Owens had laughed and had asked Waldron if Thompson knew any of the robbers, and Waldron testified that he had said he didn't know.

W. M. Reeder, a brother-in-law to King, testified that King had proposed to him in August and September that they rob a train. Reeder said he had agreed at the time, thinking it was a joke. Reeder testified he had heard Harvey King say in King's presence that "times were getting skittish" and that he, too, was in favor of robbing a train. Harvey had said they could make what money they could and leave the country. King did not speak, but Reeder testified that he had told Harvey he would not participate. Reeder also testified that King had told him at dinner on the Wednesday before the train was robbed that they were going to rob the train that night. Reeder testified he had told King to stay out of it, but King had replied that "things had gone too far." King had told him he could get the Owens boys to join him, and he had told Reeder that if he ever told anyone about the robbery, he would be killed. King and his wife, as well as W. M. Reeder, all lived in the home of Reeder's mother. Reeder testified that King had left the home the night the train was robbed about midnight and returned about 3 a.m. Reeder testified that the next morning, King had showed him three pocket knives, five shirts, a pair of socks, a pair of boots, and some money and had said that was what he got from the night before. He thought there was $160, which was inside the boots. Reeder said King had told him the others got about $11 apiece. Reeder further testified that after Harvey King was killed, King had told him where he could find Harvey's things and had told him to get them and to take the money and burn the other items. Reeder said he did not go at the time, but he had gone with the officer when he had a search warrant to where King had told him they were hidden and found them as King had told him. King's stolen items were also hidden there.

On cross-examination, Reeder testified that King never had brought the stolen items to the house but had showed them to him at their barn the next morning. Reeder denied that he was offered any reward upon the conviction of any of the robbers. He testified that King was at home until about 9 a.m. on the day that Harvey King was killed. Reeder further testified that he had gone to a baptizing at about that time of day and that Abraham Owens was also at the baptizing. Reeder said their house was about one mile from where Harvey King was killed.

A neighbor, Griffin Wright, testified for the prosecution that he had had a conversation with one of the prisoners, Charles Smith, on the Monday before the train was robbed and that Smith had told him if he would join him in a night or so that they would make at $1,000 apiece. Smith hadn't said how this could be done, and Wright testified that he had declined to go. Wright testified that he had left King's sugar mill on the Monday morning after the train had been robbed and had heard a woman's scream. Wright said he went rapidly toward the noise and saw Louisa King, a sister to Harvey and William King, running through the meadow with her bonnet off. Wright said he had gone farther and had seen King weeping over the dead body of his brother Harvey.

Dr. W. R. Bryan, a witness for the defense, said he and Thomas Hoy had heard two shots fired around 9 a.m. on the day Harvey King was murdered.

Another defense witness was Robert Henry Tuck, who had been married to King's older sister, Elenor, then deceased. Tuck testified that he had seen Abraham Owens on the day of Harvey's murder between 10 and 10:30 a.m. at a baptizing about 2½ miles from Owens's home. Tuck testified that Abraham Owens had been in the company of John Prather, and they had been about two miles from where the body of Harvey King was found.

William Owens Jr., the younger brother of Abraham and Abner Owens, testified that he had been at home the Sunday that Harvey King was killed and the previous Saturday night. He said he had slept with Abraham. He said he and Abraham would feed livestock in the mornings and did so that Sunday morning but not until after breakfast. William testified that he stayed at the house that Sunday until 9 a.m. or a little after. Abner Owens had gotten up for breakfast, and Abraham had left with John Prather. William said he and Abraham had gone to the house together after currying the horses at the stable. He said he had seen John Prather's horse at the fence before they got to the house. They had found Prather in the house, sitting down. On cross-examination, William testified that on the night Abraham was arrested, Griffin Wright had asked Abraham for Captain King's pistol. Abraham had replied that he had sent it home. William said he had taken it to King's house on Monday morning. William further testified that on Sunday morning, he and Abraham had made some cigars at the barn. Griffin Wright had asked William where Abraham was on Sunday morning, and William had replied that Abraham had been at home. Wright then had asked William if Abraham hadn't come from the direction of Captain King's house. William testified that Abraham had come through the field.

As may be recalled, Stephen Cornwell was the person who identified William King as the ringleader of the L&N robbers. Wesley Kirby testified for the defense that he had "heard some bad reports" about Cornwell having "intercourses with animals" and that "most of the people believed it to be true."

Martha Reeder, the mother-in-law of King, said King and her daughter lived at her house. She testified that on the Saturday evening before Harvey King was killed King and his wife, Ellen, had gone to see King's mother. They had returned at about 8 p.m. Mrs. Reeder further testified that King had left early Sunday morning and had returned a few minutes after 8 a.m. She said he had remained at her house until after 2 p.m. She testified that W. M. Reeder is her son and that he had told her King was at home on the night of the train robbery, but he had not said he was there all night.

R. T. Hargis, a nephew of King's, did the defense no good when he testified that he heard a conversation at King's sugar mill about robbing a train. He said King had said if he could gather ten or twelve men to rob a passenger train, that he was out of money and he did not know how to get it otherwise. Hargis testified this was some two weeks before the train was robbed. Hargis said he declined to participate in the robbery.

Louisa Reeder, a sister-in-law to King, testified that King had been at the home of Martha Reeder, his mother-in-law, on the morning that Harvey King was killed. Louisa had been in the room with him. She had gone out to see about her horse, which was about to break loose. She had been outside for about five minutes when she had heard three shots at about 9 a.m. in the direction of where Harvey King's body was found. She went into the house, and King was still there. Louisa Reeder further testified that she then had gone to the baptizing and got there about the time the baptizing had commenced. She had seen Abraham Owens there with John Prather. Reeder testified that the distance from Martha Reeder's to where Harvey King's body was found was about one mile. She said she left for the baptizing about five minutes after hearing the shots. The baptizing began about 9:30 a.m. She testified she rode in a gallop most of the way there.

Throughout the manuscript of the trial, the witnesses' words are usually recorded by the Simpson County court clerk in the third person. That is, they are paraphrased with no direct quotation. The testimony of Martha Owens—the mother of Abraham, Abner, and Billy Owens—is recorded in the usual third-person account, but before that section, there is a direct, first-person quotation in the manuscript that has been marked through by the county clerk as if it had been stricken from the record. Its content concerns the Sunday morning Harvey King was murdered and is similar to her following paraphrased testimony in the record except for this direct testimony:

"John Prather came then about 8 o'clock and he and Abe went to baptizing. King's pistol was on the fireplace that morning. I kept the pistol myself. I took it from under the bed."

Martha Owens also said her son Abner had been sick that morning and had slept until 10 a.m.

Prather, Owens's neighbor, testified that he had gone to the house of William Owens Sr. on the morning Harvey King was killed, arriving at about 8:30 a.m. Abraham Owens was not there. Prather testified that William King had come to Owens's house about five minutes after Prather had arrived. Prather said King and Abner Owens had walked out of the house about the same time King got there. Prather further testified that he had heard nothing that was said after King and Owens had left the house. Prather said King then left after about five minutes. Prather had then seen Abraham Owens arrive in the yard about five minutes after King's departure. He said he had seen Bill Owens too. Prather testified that he and Abraham Owens had gotten ready to go to the baptizing, and Abraham had told him he had to go see King. Prather said he had replied it was out of the way. Prather testified that he and Abraham had met King between Mrs. Reeder's and King's home, and that Abraham and King had had a private conversation. Prather said he was with Abraham Owens the rest of the day. He said they had arrived at the baptizing about the time the preacher was sounding the bottom of the water with a stick, which was about 10:30 a.m.

William Owens Jr. was recalled to the witness stand and testified he had slept in the same bed with Abraham Owens the night before Harvey King was killed and that their brother, Abner, had slept in the same room with them. William testified that he had been with Abraham all the morning that Harvey King was killed until Abraham had left to go with John Prather to the baptism. He said he and Abraham had fed the livestock and wrapped cigars in the barn before

Abraham and Prather had left. William said Abner Owens had not gotten up when they did. William further testified that he had been at home the night Abraham Owens was arrested. Griffin Wright had asked Abraham where Captain King's pistol was and he replied that he did not have it, that he had sent it back to King on Monday morning with William, who told Wright this was true.

Testimony from all witnesses concluded on Monday, January 14. Closing arguments were made by both sides of counsel on Tuesday, Wednesday, and Thursday of that week. At that point, Judge Rogers gave instructions to the jury. Included in those instructions was that even if all ten defendants had sworn an oath that whoever talked about who was involved in the derailment and robbery of the Louisville & Nashville Railroad train would be killed, only those defendants who had actually killed Harvey King or had prior knowledge that Harvey King was to be murdered or who had otherwise aided or assisted in the killing of Harvey King could be convicted of murder.

At this point, Judge Rogers turned the case over to the jury late Thursday evening. The jury reached a verdict Saturday morning, which was delivered before the court and the ten defendants. Eight of the defendants were found not guilty of the murder of Harvey King. Captain William P. King and Abraham Owens were found guilty of his murder.

According to *Railroad Robbers or the Life of King and Owens*, King and Owens were sent back to jail to await Judge Rogers's sentencing the following Wednesday. The prosecution said they were prepared to proceed to try the remaining prisoners on the charges of derailing and robbing the train. The defense said they were not prepared and asked for the case to be continued until the June term of the circuit court, which was granted, and the judge set bail for the remaining eight defendants at $2,500 each. According to the Louisville *Courier*, Wesley Finn, William Finn, David Wainscott, and Joseph Payne were released on bail. Abner Owens, Charles Smith, John Colbert, and Robert Hoy could not make bail.

On Monday, January 21, attorneys for King and Owens asked for a new trial, which Judge Rogers refused on the grounds that they were given a fair trial with adequate assistance of counsel. The attorneys then notified the court that they would be taking the case to the Court of Appeals.

King and Owens appeared before Judge Rogers on Wednesday, January 23 for sentencing. Judge Rogers sentenced the men to be hanged by the neck until dead on March 22.

According to Ditto's book, after the judge passed sentence, Abraham Owens asked for permission to speak to the prosecuting attorney, which the judge granted. Owens addressed Judge Loving while another of the prosecuting attorneys, John A. Finn, stood near him: "Judge, I charge you with pleading my life away, and my advice to you is never to prosecute another innocent man while you live. You too, Mr. Finn." Loving replied, "Young man, you have endeavored to give me advice. Now I wish to give you some, and that is, you had better prepare to meet your God, for I believe from the bottom of my heart that you are the very man who killed Harvey King, and you ought to and will hang, sure." Finn replied, "I have endeavored to discharge my duty as a lawyer and have a clear conscience on that subject."

In February, the Court of Appeals denied King's and Owens's appeals.

Also in February, Lieutenant Colonel Samuel F. Johnson, of the 52nd Regiment of the Kentucky Mounted Infantry during the Civil War and the commanding officer of Captain King and Private Abner Owens, wrote a letter to Governor Thomas E. Bramlette, praising the bravery and dedication of King and Owens in fighting against Confederate guerrillas both during and after the war. Abraham's brother Abner was still in prison for robbery and train derailment. While saying their military service was no excuse for their crimes, Johnson asserted it may be considered a reason for the governor to consider executive clemency in their case. A reporter for the Louisville *Courier* had written of the lieutenant colonel the previous month:

"I do not know whether it is proper or not to speak of it but will say that Wm. P. King and Abner Owens were members of the 52nd Kentucky Federal regiment and were thoroughly tutored in the art of robbing by the Lieutenant Colonel of that regiment, Samuel Johnson, an ex-Methodist preacher, but while in command here could swear louder and bet higher than anybody."

The Vidette of Hartsville, Tennessee, confusing the convicted murderer Abraham Owens with his imprisoned brother Abner Owens, similarly wrote of Lieutenant Colonel Johnson:

"They (Owens and King), no doubt, learned their first lessons in robbery and murder from the graceless scoundrel who commanded them during the war— the psalm-singing cut-throat Johnson—the ex-Colonel of the 52d Kentucky, who since the close of the war has been the patient recipient of more kicks and curses than any provost-hero of his rank."

In fact, because he had mentioned Abraham Owens by name in his letter to Governor Bramlette, Johnson was also confused about which Owens brother had served under Captain King. Abraham Owens served four years in Company H, 5th Kentucky Cavalry, not in the 52nd Kentucky as did his brother and King.

Bramlette refused to pardon King and Owens or to commute their sentence.

The Reverend L. M. Horn, a minister from Franklin who had visited King and Abraham Owens frequently during their incarceration, went to the state capital along with Ellen Reeder King, King's wife, and Mary Newman King, his mother. Reverend Horn told the governor that the condemned men were not in the proper spiritual condition to face execution. Bramlette extended the day of their execution until May 17.

Meanwhile, this bought more time for King and Abraham Owens to try to escape. The prisoners were allowed frequent visits from friends, and many of these friends brought them tools to cut through the wooden floor of their cell. Other prisoners were in the cell with them and helped King and Owens in their subterfuge by lying on a bed during the day, which covered the hole in the floor. This attempt at escape was foiled when the prisoners discovered impenetrable limestone rock beneath the wooden flooring.

A second escape was devised in which the prisoners planned to rush the jailer and guards as their supper dishes were taken from their cell for washing. King, Abraham Owens, and John Colbert, who was waiting for his trial for robbery and obstructing the railroad track, knew this would be the best time of day to attempt such an escape because nighttime would be fast-approaching. According to Ditto, the procedure for meals was that the jailer would bring the dishes in or out of the cells while a guard of about six or seven men formed a half-circle just outside the cell.

On Tuesday, April 11, the jailer had his hands full with the supper dishes and was opening the cell door when Abraham Owens jumped over the jailer, surprising the guards in the narrow hallway outside the cell. The soldiers were unable to shoot or bayonet without fear of wounding or killing their own men. Owens was followed quickly outside of the cell by King and Colbert. The guards tried to hit the prisoners with the butt of their guns but failed. Soon, the three prisoners were outside the walls while the relief guard commenced firing. King and Owens headed in one direction, while Colbert took another route.

A military camp was situated about fifty yards away and joined in the pursuit. Owens jumped over a fence and hid under a kitchen but was found and returned to jail. King also leaped over a fence but was shot in the left arm. He made it about a half-mile from the jail before being captured and returned. Colbert was apprehended around the same time.

According to *Railroad Robbers or the Life of King and Owens*, King's wound was examined, and it was discovered that a bone between the elbow and the wrist was broken with about one inch of that bone gone, but because the other bone was intact, his arm would not have to be amputated. Still thinking of escaping the hangman's noose, King asked the doctor if the wound would cripple him for life. The doctor assured him it would not. It was while King was suffering through the pain from this wound that he mentioned they had attempted to escape from jail previously. This was news to the jailer and guards, but when they examined the cell, they found augurs, saws, and other tools that showed they would have been successful previously if they had not run into limestone.

On Tuesday, May 14, a mere three days before the rescheduled execution, Ellen Reeder King; Mary Newman King; William Owens Sr., Abraham Owens's father; and a member of the defense team traveled to Frankfort to see Governor Bramlette. They presented the governor with documents that Ellen Reeder King would have evidence before the June term of the Simpson County Circuit Court that would show the innocence of the convicted men and earn them a new trial. The governor extended the men's execution date a second time, this time to June 28.

On Monday and Tuesday of that week, Sheriff Ira J. Bogan had been selecting a site for the construction of the gallows for the Friday hangings. Such activity ended when Ellen Reeder King presented Bogan with the governor's second respite of the execution.

It was reported in Ditto's book that Captain King had told the prisoners' spiritual advisers that if the two were hanged, one innocent man (King) and one guilty man (Owens) would be hanged for the murder of Harvey King. Undermining King's testimony at even this late stage was his insistence that he also was not involved in the robbery and derailment of the train, even though he was identified by at least ten witnesses who were on the train.

In the meantime, the June term of the Simpson County Circuit Court was called to order by Judge Rogers on Tuesday, June 18, and resumed with the business of the prosecution of the robbery of the L&N Railroad train. The attorneys for the prisoners said they were ready to defend King and Abraham Owens on the robbery charge. An attorney for the prosecution, C. W. Milliken, responded: "Your Honor, I should like to know the propriety of trying men already found guilty and under sentence of a greater crime. I therefore dismiss the indictment as it relates to William P. King and Abraham Owens." The attorneys for the defense then asked for a continuance of the cases against the remaining eight defendants on the grounds that several important witnesses were absent. Judge Rogers responded that he had given them ample time to be ready for trial. At this point, the cases were called.

Charles Smith arose and addressed the court and said he wished to submit his case, provided that he could make a statement before pleading guilty. The judge granted his request.

Smith said:

> "Gentlemen of the jury, I plead guilty to being one among the party that robbed the train on the Louisville & Nashville railroad. I was drunk at the time, and the greater number engaged in it were acquaintances of mine and took advantage of my condition and drew me into it. While the robbery was being committed, I was too much intoxicated to take any part in the affair and was barely able to reach home. I received none of the plunder or money. I therefore humbly beg your clemency as well as that of the court and leave this plain statement with you and submit the case to the court."

The jury deliberated a few minutes and sentenced Smith to three years in prison, which the judge passed accordingly.

At this, the defense asked for a continuance for the other defendants. The judge granted an extension until the next circuit court, which would be the first Monday in September. He told defense counsel that if the witnesses did not appear at the September term, the remaining defendants would be tried anyway.

No evidence was presented by Ellen Reeder King to the June circuit court that would clear her husband of his murder conviction.

However, before the June term was adjourned, counsel for King and Owens submitted an affidavit signed by one of King's sisters that said Riley Towe, who had testified in the murder trial against King and Owens, had been the one to have killed Harvey King. Esquire Wright, a magistrate in Simpson County, then swore out a warrant for the arrest of Riley Towe for murder, and Joseph Payne and Wesley Finn, two of the defendants in the robbery case who were out of jail on bail, were sent to apprehend Towe.

This happened on Thursday, June 20, and Towe was then living in nearby Allen County, Kentucky. Towe had been forewarned that a warrant was out for his arrest and feared that he would be killed by Payne and Wesley Finn for resisting arrest. Towe hid from Payne and Finn until the following Monday when eight men from Franklin came to his rescue before he could be arrested for murder. Once

Towe made it to Franklin under the protection of friends, no one chose to enforce the warrant.

On Saturday, June 22, citizens of Franklin sent Governor Bramlette a letter informing him of the current situation in hopes that he would not be misled into granting a third respite from execution to King and Owens.

***

A reporter from the Louisville *Courier*, along with several ministers and Sheriff Ira J. Bogan, met with William King and Abraham Owens on Tuesday, June 25.

During the meeting, one of the ministers said to King and Owens: "You cannot live but a few days longer, for next Friday terminates the period of time limited for the second gubernatorial respite, and under all the circumstances of the case, with the present lights before you, it is unreasonable to expect executive clemency a third time to be further manifested in your favor."

Owens replied: "No, I do not. In fact, I did not expect it before. I am innocent of the crime for which I must so soon die. Although I am not afraid to die, yet I dread the manner of my death. I am free to confess that there are some objects that make life dear, and it is a fearful thing, on such a sudden summons, to be called to the tomb, but I shall meet death upon the scaffold with whatever degree of composure I may possess, solemnly protesting with my latest breath that I am innocent of, and had no complicity in, the death of Harvey King."

King replied: "I, too, am innocent of the crime for which I have been convicted and sentenced to be hanged. I have suffered much, but it grieves me most that I must leave this world with the charge of fratricide resting upon my name and family. No one loved his brother more than I did mine, and I would at any time have lain down my life in the defense of his. Yet I am on Friday to be hanged as his murderer."

***

The *Nashville Union and American* newspaper described the incongruity of Friday, June 28, 1867, in Franklin, Kentucky: "The birds were sweetly warbling in the trees and a cool breeze swept over the broad green landscape, giving promise of a lovely day." William P. King had been visited nearly all day Thursday by his wife and his mother and two sisters. Abraham Owens was likewise visited in the cell by his mother, a sister and a brother.

At 9 a.m., Sheriff Bogan and a company of twenty-two armed citizen guards marched to the jail, while a detachment of twelve guards of the 2nd U.S. Infantry filed off to leave the two prisoners in the hands of the civil authorities and citizen guards. Meanwhile, inside the jail, King and Owens were singing and praying with five ministers.

A little before 11 a.m., the prisoners had ropes placed around their necks and had their hands bound together by leather straps, secured by buckles. The two condemned prisoners said goodbye to their fellow prisoners. Abraham Owens told his brother Abner to hold his head and die like a man if he had to die. Sheriff Bogan asked Owens if he wanted his coat collar to be turned to where the rope couldn't be seen, but Owens replied that he was proud to wear the rope and wished it to be seen.

A little after eleven, the procession to the gallows began and was headed by the Franklin Cornet band, which the prisoners had requested. It played a funeral march all the way to the place of execution about a half a mile outside of town next to the railroad track. None of the citizens of Franklin had wanted the gallows to be built upon their property, so it was constructed within three feet of the track on property owned by the Louisville & Nashville Railroad Company.

Following the brass band in the procession was the 2nd U.S. Infantry under Lieutenant Maize. Thereafter followed a wagon containing King and Owens, the sheriff, and clergy. Then came another wagon with two coffins covered by a quilt. At the end of the procession were the citizen guards, followed by about 6,000 citizens, many of them female. The procession arrived at the scaffold at about noon.

Owens was the first man on the scaffold, followed by King, the sheriff, the five ministers, and members of the press, who were provided seats on the scaffold. At the request of the prisoners, "We're Going Home to Die No More" was sung, with both King and Owens joining in the singing, and after a prayer by the Reverend J. F. Redford of the Methodist church, the prisoners were told they were allowed twenty minutes each to speak. The prisoners asked that their arms be released while they spoke, but their request was denied. Sheriff Bogan introduced King first. As reported in the *Nashville Union and American*, King spoke before the silent crowd:

My Dying Friends: I see here today many of my old acquaintances and friends. We never before met on such an occasion as this. Eight months ago, my dying friends, I was as free as any man now standing before me. I have only a few minutes to live and then I will be called upon to die the most honorable death that a man can die. But I can die with as good grace as any man. God witnesses my innocence, and though I am, on the gallows, I could take my bitterest enemy, who swore against me, and love him. Thank God I have a hope beyond the gallows, a home in heaven. I would like to talk a good deal, but my health will not permit. I have been buffeted from one place to another, but I hope now to be for once a free man. I am here with you now, and I hope that in a few hours, I shall be with my father in paradise.

Peace within a man's heart is the greatest consolation that can be afforded. He can lay down and sleep at night and nothing crosses his breast. I mean by that, the man who sets the example of a Christian. Do that and you can lay down in the most humble place if you have the Savior's love and peace.

Since I have been in jail, I have been like a wild animal in the forest. My mind has been directed to my dear mother, my loved sisters, and my darling wife. Since I was taken from them, I have never been able to be a free man. I have done all I could to be a free man.

Oh, if I could only be at home once more! It would be the happiest moment of my life. But if it is the will of the great

Jehovah that I should die, I'm the happiest man in the world. I'm bound to go to heaven. You may swear this on me and take away my life, but you can't take away my soul. Thank God, I have a friend and redeemer in Heaven!

I have not studied to make this speech and don't want to weary your patience. If I had the strength and voice I once had, I could talk to this crowd. I want you to forsake your sins and meet me in Heaven. Tell Griff Wright I want to meet him in Heaven. Yes, Griff, you promised to stand to me and to be true and faithful, but you forsook me and plunged me as deep as you could. You hunted all the testimony in the courts of Simpson County.

I'm as innocent of my brother's death as any man here. I said Abe Owens done it, and you hang me with what testimony you get against me. I'll never stand before you again, and all I can say is, meet me in Heaven, where no trials, no troubles, no sorrows ever reach.

I am today a poor worm of the dust. I am here only a few minutes, and you will see me no more. I want to leave the world and leave it happy and in glory and honor, and I want you to tell your children that I died like a man. It may be the Lord's will for me to hang today. It may put an end to murder in your county. Why should I say so? The little boys are growing up, and they can say a man was hung because he was a murderer. It has been said and sung that I've been one of the bloodiest men that ever lived. While in the service I have killed men in self-defense but never in cold blood. If I've said anything to hurt the feelings of anyone here, I wish to be pardoned, but I cannot take it back.

I'm to go up before my God, and I would not stand on this scaffold and tell you a lie. If I was guilty I'd tell it, but I'm as innocent of the death of my brother as any man can be. Great love existed between me and my brother. There is not a person within the sound of my voice who loves their brothers better than I did mine, and had I known who killed him I should have avenged his death. I would rather have left the continent of America than to do it. If I'd been guilty of the death of my brother, I wouldn't have been hung here today; I'd have been too sharp for that. I knew not till I saw my brother's body that he was dead. I'm proud to say that I would have killed the man who did it. I loved my brother and would have fought for him to the death. I never knew him to have a fuss with anyone without looking to me for protection. I'm as innocent as Tobe Procter or Art Wilson over there. I'll tell you why I said Abe Owens had done it. I had seen the blood on his pistol, and I am proud that I said it.

It is better for a man to die guilty than innocent. A guilty man can say he deserved to die, but it is a hard thing to take an innocent man from his family forever.

I would to God that in the hour I found my brother, he could have told me who killed him. I wouldn't have asked civil law to prove it. I said I believed Abe Owens was guilty of my brother's death, and let him defend himself if he can. But Mr. Owens says he is not guilty, and I don't know today who did it.

I have to die and will never meet you on earth again. I don't want to say anything against you, but if I am going to the place I hope to, I'd rather do it than stay here with you. I would to God I had died when I was an infant or at some other time before this thing commenced. Eight months ago, I had as little idea of being hung as you. It's only a momentary pang to be hung. It's soon over with. But thank God, I have a hope beyond the gallows and the grave.

I've been like the balance of you and done wrong as well. I know I have and confess it, but let him who is without sin throw the first stone. The best happiness is the life of a Christian. If you call him a thief or a murderer, it does not make it so. I have confessed my sins and now look to God for glory and a crown in the happy home I will soon reach. I'm sure to go to Heaven. I feel that I am on my way to glory. I love you and would to God you could feel as I do.

I want to meet you all in Heaven. Tell my neighbors and friends that the last words of Bill King were that they should meet him in Heaven. Go home and reflect upon your sins, for you don't know how soon you may share Bill King's fate. Go home and read your Bibles. Be good Christians. I love you all and would not hurt a hair on your heads. I give you this advice as you must one day appear before the Great Judge. I hope to meet you in Heaven. Goodbye.

Abraham Owens spoke next:

My Friends: I'm here today to make you a speech. It is a thing I never before undertook. I have no education and can barely read and write a little. I am, and always was, a little bashful. I would like to know why I am here. Is there a man on the ground who can say I am to be executed for murder today?

I have fought for my country and now have to die with the name of a traitor. I am accused of robbing railroads and murdering my neighbor boy. Have you brought any proof that I am a murderer? Can you prove that I had a particle of a part in it? Thank God, I was not here when the war was going on and ever pestered anyone in this country. I was in the service three years and six months and done as good duty as any man. And I can say before God that if ever I shot or murdered a man, I don't know it.

So far as the statement is that Billy King had come and told me to kill his brother and that I went and told him where to find his brother, it is not so, gentlemen. If I had intended to kill him, I would never had such a conversation. I never knew Harvey King was dead till Monday evening. How did I hear it? My little brother and sister came from school and told me he was dead. They tried to prove that I never went near the corpse. When I went over there, my mother said to go back home and come tomorrow. I did come next morning and stayed there till he was buried.

I borrowed a pistol from Billy King to go and visit some friends in Tennessee. When Sunday came, I was late in getting up and Billy King came over to see my father about cattle getting into his corn. He wanted me to go to church with him and I went though I turned to go to Tennessee. My horse was not shod behind, and I gave up going. Did I have a pistol on this day? No, you can't prove it.

It is a money speculation in human blood that now takes away my life. What is $1,000? Why, $1,000 will buy two men's lives now a days. The pistol went home on Monday morning; had it ever been shot? My brother started to school and got to the evaporator. He met Billy King, who took down the pistol and when he started away, the little boy took the pistol. How many hands did that pistol pass through? I can suffer with the greatest of grace. It is better for me to die innocent than guilty. You may say today, Abe Owens told a lie upon the scaffold. I believe it not. I say before God and man, I did not know Harvey King was dead. I admit I've been a sinner and a gambler and very bad man, but I think I have forgiveness for my sins, and I think I'm better off today than some who swore to a lie. I say before God and man that Griff Wright swore to a lie. When two good witnesses besides a man's friends will not be taken, I'd rather die. Captain (R. P.) Finn, say to Griff Wright that he swore to a lie but forgive him. He was the first man who tried to get me to robbing.

There's Cornwell, who turned state's evidence. He swore my foot was crushed while another man says I was the second in the train. I've written a little history and don't think it necessary to explain the railroad robbery any further.

Both men spoke far beyond their allotted twenty minutes of time. Shortly before 2 p.m., Lieutenant Maize of the 2nd U.S. Infantry informed Sheriff Bogan that if the speaking wasn't stopped in five minutes, he would withdraw the troops. The speaking thus concluded and was followed by prayer and singing.

King and Owens shook hands with those around them and with each other. They only requested that the sheriff see that they not fall too far. White caps were drawn over their heads. The brass band, as requested by the prisoners, played the "Death March." Sheriff Bogan adjusted the ropes and said, "I will count five. Now be ready. One, two, three, four, five." The trap door sprung open at 2 p.m. Owens's neck was broken, and he died almost instantly. King appeared to be slowly strangling, and his body convulsed for five minutes before it became motionless. At this, their bodies were removed for burial.

***

ABRAHAM OWENS.

Capt. Wm. P. KING.

William King and Abraham Owens lie in Blackjack Cemetery in Franklin, Kentucky. An artist drew their likeness in jail after their unsuccessful escape.

Wesley Finn (right) as an old man next to a photo of his father, Peter Finn. Peter Finn bailed his son out of jail before his trial on train robbery and derailment charges. Wesley Finn left Kentucky for Arkansas and changed his name. Peter Finn declared bankruptcy.

TO DIE NO MORE

N o one had been tried for the train robbery or derailment. Charles Smith had pleaded guilty and sentenced to three years in the penitentiary, but that had been all.

The defense attorneys made mention before the judge in June that they would seek a change of venue if they could get an affidavit to that effect, stating that it was impossible to get a fair trial in Simpson County. This they did at the September term of the Simpson County Circuit Court, and the judge granted a change of venue to nearby Logan County for the November term.

At the September term in Simpson County, Peter Finn, the father of Wesley Finn, acknowledged that he was indebted for $4,000 to the Commonwealth of Kentucky that both Wesley Finn and Abner Owens would appear at the November term of the Logan County Circuit Court. Neither Wesley Finn nor Abner Owens appeared in November.

It was soon learned by the Simpson County Circuit Court that Peter Finn had sold approximately two hundred acres of land to two of his brothers and a son, Alfred J. Finn. This transaction took place on October 15, and it was intimated that all parties knew that Wesley Finn and Abner Owens had or would soon be leaving the Commonwealth of Kentucky for parts unknown. Peter Finn had sold fifty acres of his property to his brother Abraham Finn for $500. He sold sixty acres of land to his brother John W. Finn for $915. He sold a twenty-five-acre tract of land for $500 and a separate twenty-five-acre tract for $400 to his son Alfred J. Finn. (Peter Finn would give the remaining forty acres to his son King Loving Finn in December.)

W. B. Thompson, attorney for the commonwealth, filed a petition in equity in Simpson Circuit Court in November to declare this sale of land void and for the commonwealth to sell the property and retain enough money to cover Peter Finn's debt, interest, and taxes of the amount owed to the commonwealth. (The petition in equity would later be amended to include King Loving Finn.)

Peter Finn declared bankruptcy in U.S. District Court in December.

The commonwealth's attorney took the depositions in January and February 1868 of several townspeople about their knowledge of the whereabouts of Wesley Finn and Abner Owens on October 15, 1867, when Peter Finn sold land to Alfred J., Abraham, and John W. Finn. Griff Wright testified that John W. Finn told him prior to October 15 that Abner Owens and Wesley Finn had gone and "never would be seen here again." Wright testified that the four Finn defendants were all related to each other, and that Wesley Finn and Abner Owens lived in the neighborhood with them.

Another Simpson County resident, C. W. Holland, testified in his deposition that all four Finn defendants knew that Wesley Finn and Abner Owens had fled the country before the 15th of October.

C. W. Milliken, an attorney who helped successfully prosecute William King and Abraham Owens for murder, testified in his deposition of having seen Peter Finn in the Simpson County court clerk's office on October 15, 1867:

I was in the county court clerk's office about the time referred to and found Peter Finn, his wife, and Bill Hail, county clerk. There, I told Peter Finn that I had learned he was selling off his land and asked him if it was so. He made no answer. I then called his name and asked him again, telling him that I was talking to him. He made no reply. I then told him that we would fight any transfer he might make to the bitter end. He made no reply but asked the clerk if he was done with him. He then left the room. I think on the same day I met J. W. Finn who asked me what about his purchase of Peter's land. Whether or not it was good and whether there would be a lawsuit about it. I told him there would be a lawsuit, that we intended to attack the sale as fraudulent, and he was only buying a lawsuit. He said then he believed he would have nothing to do with it, that Peter was owing him was his reason for buying.

Milliken further testified that it was his understanding that Wesley Finn and Abner Owens had fled the country by October 15 and "that impression seemed to be general." Milliken added that Alfred J., John W., and Abraham Finn live in the neighborhood of Peter Finn and did so at that time as well.

B. W. Hail, Simpson County court clerk, testified in his deposition to the commonwealth's attorney that it was "pretty generally reported" that Wesley Finn and Abner Owens had left the country before the land deeds were acknowledged.

Alfred J. Finn, John W. Finn, and Abraham Finn filed an answer in March in Simpson Circuit Court that they did not know that Wesley Finn and Abner Owens had fled the country when they made the land purchase from Peter Finn. It was also in March that the Commonwealth of Kentucky added King Loving Finn, a son of Peter Finn, to the equity petition in Simpson Circuit Court.

In September in Simpson Circuit Court, a judgment was rendered in which the sale of the two hundred acres of land from Peter Finn and his wife to John W. Finn, Abraham Finn, Alfred J. Finn, and King Loving Finn was cancelled. The land was then to be sold at the Simpson County Courthouse to the highest bidder, retaining enough money to cover Peter Finn's debt, interest, and taxes of the amount owed to the commonwealth.

The land was sold to John A. Finn, one of the lawyers who had successfully prosecuted King and Owens for murder, at public auction at the courthouse door in Franklin in October for $2,011. However, this sale was set aside in March 1869 in Simpson Circuit Court because John A. Finn asked for the protection of the court because he could not get a title to the land he bought from King Loving Finn. The court then cancelled the sale of the property to John A. Finn (and W. W. Bush, another of the lawyers who had prosecuted King and Owens).

In addition, at the March 1869 term of the Simpson Circuit Court, the court rendered judgment that the two hundred acres of land owned by Peter Finn be sold by tract and then sold in gross before the Simpson County Courthouse door to the highest bidder. The money from the sale of the land would first be paid to cover Peter Finn's debt, interest, and taxes owed to the Commonwealth of Kentucky. The court declared that at the next term, it would decide whether the sale money should be given directly to the assignee in bankruptcy for Peter Finn—E. L. Hines—or whether the sale money would be appropriated first to the Commonwealth of Kentucky. Any money left over after the payment of this debt would then be held by E. L. Hines.

The Wesley Finn/Abner Owens cases weren't the only ones called in Logan County Circuit Court in November 1867. John Colbert also appeared in court on the charges of obstructing the Louisville & Nashville Railroad track and robbing the L&N train. He was convicted on both counts, and Judge George C. Rogers followed the recommendation of the separate juries and sentenced him to seven years at hard labor in the state penitentiary for robbing the passenger train, and after that sentence was served, another eight years of hard labor in the state penitentiary for obstructing the L&N Railroad track.

It was never made clear why the remaining four accused men who weren't dead (Captain King, Harvey King, and Abraham Owens), in prison (Charles Smith and John Colbert), free after turning state's evidence (Stephen Cornwell and John Evans), or on the lam (Wesley Finn and Abner Owens) didn't also appear to face charges in the train robbery and track obstruction. Nevertheless, the record never shows an appearance by Robert Hoy, William E. Finn, Joseph Payne, or David R. Wainscott in court. In fact, in the 1870 federal census for Simpson County, John Colbert, William E. Finn, and David Wainscott are listed as farmers who had families. Robert Hoy was also listed as living in Simpson County, having a family, and working as a blacksmith, the trade of his former master, Thomas Hoy, from whom he took his last name. William E. Finn is often listed as being the brother of Wesley Finn. William E. Finn was the son of Daniel Finn, who was a brother to Peter Finn, the father of Wesley Finn. Joseph Payne is apparently lost to history.

Abner Owens is also lost to history. It is written in a family history that he was killed out West, a template to be used for a few souls of Simpson County who left this world unaccounted for at that time.

Stephen Cornwell, who was the person who identified William King as the ringleader of the L&N robbers, is listed in the 1870 federal census as having moved back to his birthplace, Macon County, Tennessee. He eventually married and had eight children. He lived to be 84 and was a postmaster there for a period of time. Macon County had also been the birthplace of William King and Abraham Owens.

Wesley Finn moved to Mundell, Arkansas, and changed his name to John White. His first wife, Sarah Caruthers Finn, whom he married in 1866, divorced Wesley Finn/John White in Jasper, Missouri, in 1868. He married Rebecca Jane Coker in Carroll County, Arkansas, in June 1868, and they had a dozen children. He was buried in Carroll County, but in the 1960s a dam was constructed that created a lake that covered the Mundell area, so his grave was moved to Garfield, Arkansas, in Benton County. He had been a sergeant in Company F, 52nd Kentucky Mounted Infantry during the Civil War, serving under William P. King.

It all comes back in this tragic story to Captain King. It was his idea to rob the Louisville & Nashville Railroad. It was his gun that killed Harvey King. And it comes back to Ellen Reeder King, whom King married in 1866 and widowed in 1867 by his own misdeeds.

Ellen had remarried and was living in her mother's home with her new husband, George W. Coltharp, at the time of the 1870 federal census. They had their own home in Franklin by the time of the 1880 census and had three children, ages nine, six, and three. George Coltharp died in 1880, and Ellen married Archibald Hunt in Franklin in 1887, a marriage that lasted until Archibald's death in 1912. The 1920 federal census lists Ellen living with her son, Thomas M. Coltharp, and his family in Crowley County, Colorado. Ellen was buried in Crowley County in 1927.

Probably the most tragic of all the figures is Mary Newman King. She not only lost a son, Harvey, to murder in 1866, but she lost another son, William, to death by hanging in 1867. Between those deaths, a daughter, Rachel Casey, died. These deaths followed the accidental shooting and killing of her husband, Peter King, in 1864. A daughter, Ellen King Tuck, had died in 1860, and another son, Jonathan Newman King, was shot and killed during the Civil War in 1865. That's six deaths in a seven-year period in one family, most of them violent deaths.

Ellen King Tuck and Jonathan Newman King were not only siblings, but they were married to siblings. Ellen King Tuck was married to Robert Henry Tuck, who testified in the King/Owens murder trial, and Jonathan Newman King was married to Nancy Tuck King, Robert Henry's younger sister. Robert Henry Tuck had also been a sergeant in Company F, 52nd Kentucky Mounted Infantry during the Civil War, serving under William P. King.

Jonathan Newman King had a life story almost as turbulent as his younger brothers, William and Harvey. Instead of joining the Union army, Jonathan was a Confederate soldier, joining the 48th Alabama Regiment in April 1862. He fought at Sharpsburg and at Fredericksburg. The record shows he was discharged in Lynchburg, Virginia. Jonathan resided with his wife and three children in Granby, Missouri, when the war began. He worked there as a miner. In his book, Ditto writes that Jonathan King was killed in Missouri in 1865 by Kansas Jayhawkers. William King went to Missouri to return his brother's body to Kentucky.

After her husband's death, Nancy Tuck King returned with her children to live with her parents in her birthplace of Lafayette, Tennessee, according to the 1870 federal census. The 1880 census shows that Nancy Tuck King and her youngest child lived with her brother, Robert Henry Tuck, in Franklin, Kentucky. Nancy King died in Polk County, Florida, in 1917.

***

The prosecution never accused William King of shooting Harvey King. They accused him of supplying the pistol to Abraham Owens, who then used it to shoot Harvey King. So the focus is on where was Abraham Owens on the Sunday morning Harvey King was killed.

A neighbor, William Welty, testified that he heard three gun or pistol shots in quick succession at about 9 o'clock that morning. Welty said the sound of gunfire came from the direction of where Harvey King's body was found. Another neighbor, John Hendrick, also testified that he heard three shots in rapid succession at 9 a.m. that day. Dr. W. R. Bryan testified that he and Thomas Hoy heard two shots fired around 9 a.m. that Sunday. Louisa Reeder testified she was outside that morning and heard three shots at about 9 a.m. in the direction of where Harvey King's body was found. She also said Captain King, who lived in the home of her mother with his wife, was inside the house at that time.

On cross-examination by the defense, W. M. Reeder, a brother-in-law to King, testified that King was at home about 9 a.m. on the morning Harvey King was killed. Reeder also testified that he went to a baptizing at that time of day, and Abraham Owens was at the baptism. Louisa Reeder, a sister to W. M. Reeder, said she left for the baptizing about five minutes after hearing the shots at 9 a.m. She testified that the baptizing began about 9:30 a.m. She said she saw Abraham Owens there, and John Prather was with him. She testified, "We went in a gallop most of the way." This testimony recalls Abraham Owens's statement on the gallows: "When two good witnesses besides a man's friends will not be taken, I'd rather die."

As mentioned earlier, John Prather testified that he had arrived at the home of William Owens Sr. at about 8:30 a.m. on the Sunday that Harvey King was killed. He said Abraham Owens was not there when he got there. Prather testified that Captain King had arrived at the house about five minutes after Prather got there and came into the Owens home. Prather said King and Abner Owens had left the house and had a private conversation outside. This testimony would be consistent with Ditto's book, quoting King as saying he went that Sunday morning to the home of William Owens Sr. to tell him to keep his cattle out of his cornfield, and not finding Owens at home, gave his son Abner Owens the message.

Prather further testified that King had left about five minutes after arriving and that Abraham Owens and Bill Owens had arrived about five minutes after King had left their home. Prather said he and Abraham Owens then got ready to go to the baptizing. Prather testified that Abraham Owens had told him he had to go see King, and Prather had replied that would be out of the way. Prather had said they met King between Mrs. Reeder's home where King lived and King's mother's home. Prather testified that King and Abraham Owens had a private conversation. This, too, is consistent with Ditto's book, where he quotes King as saying he was getting wood that Sunday morning and Abraham Owens and "a young man by the name of Prather" met him. According to King, Abraham Owens said, "I will return your pistol tomorrow morning by my small brother." To which King said he replied, "All right," before Prather and Abraham Owens rode away. This is further confirmed by Owens's statement on the gallows: "I borrowed a pistol from Billy King to go and visit some friends in Tennessee. When Sunday came, I was late in getting up and Billy King came over to see my father about cattle getting into his corn. He wanted me to go to church with him and I went though I turned to go to Tennessee. My horse was not shod behind, and I gave up going." Owens can be excused for confusing going to the baptizing with King instead of Prather because he was about to be hanged in a matter of minutes. Otherwise, his statement also rings true.

Prather concluded his testimony by saying that he and Abraham Owens got to the baptizing about the time the "preacher was sounding the water or bottom with a stick," which was about 10:30 a.m. Prather said he was with Abraham Owens the rest of the day.

Robert Henry Tuck also confirmed he saw Abraham Owens and Prather between 10 and 10:30 a.m. at the baptizing. Tuck testified that the baptizing was about 2½ miles from Owens's home and about two miles from where Harvey King's body was found.

William Owens Jr. testified that Abraham Owens stayed at their home until about 9 a.m. or a little after. William said he was with Abraham all the morning that Harvey King was killed until Abraham left to go with Prather to the baptism.

Then there's Martha Owens's testimony of the whereabouts of the pistol that Sunday morning: "John Prather came then about 8 o'clock and he and Abe went to the baptizing. King's pistol was on the fireplace that morning. I kept the pistol myself. I took it from under the bed." That testimony was stricken from the record although it can still be read in the manuscript of the trial. Why was this testimony stricken? Yes, it comes from the mother of Abraham Owens, but the jury could certainly take into account that these words came from a mother whose son's life was on the line. The jury could believe her or not, but her testimony deserved to be preserved. According to the Louisville *Courier*, Abraham Owens protested to Judge Rogers on the day he was sentenced that he hadn't received a fair trial. One of the reasons he gave was the way his family's testimony had been treated in court. Obviously, the attorneys for the commonwealth were expected to impeach the testimony from the Owens family as much as possible, but to have testimony that is possibly mitigating to the defense dismissed from the record gives credence to Abraham Owens's complaint.

Another aspect of the trial that Abraham Owens protested to the judge on the day of sentencing was that he had not been able to consult freely with defense counsel. Yes, all ten of the accused were in court during the proceedings, but Owens's complaint was that he had otherwise been in jail the rest of the time and didn't have sufficient opportunity to speak to his lawyers outside of the courtroom. Certainly, Owens would have told his attorneys to hit harder on the timeline of his whereabouts on the Sunday morning that Harvey King was murdered. In itself, the testimony given about where Abraham Owens was at 9 a.m. on that fateful morning could be enough to create reasonable doubt among the jury.

So who killed Harvey King? Although William King believed that Abraham Owens had killed his brother when he saw the blood on his gun he had lent Owens, by the time King was on the gallows, he said Owens said he didn't murder Harvey King. King's last statement was that he didn't know who killed his brother. It wasn't the job of the defense to find who killed Harvey King, only to prove that

Owens didn't do it and thereby prove that King didn't provide the murder weapon to Owens to commit the murder.

After both Owens and King were convicted of murder, the defense made a desperate attempt to prove that Riley Towe had committed the murder. But before the convictions, it was up to the Commonwealth of Kentucky to prove that Abraham Owens did it and that he was provided the weapon to do so by Captain King.

If Captain King didn't know who killed Harvey King, did Abraham Owens know?

BEYOND THE GRAVE

I mentioned earlier that Abner Owens, younger brother to Abraham, "was killed out West, a template to be used for a few souls of Simpson County who left this world unaccounted for at that time."

There is a more intriguing story about the youngest of the Owens brothers, William Owens Jr. It was reported in the October 10, 1907, edition of The Franklin (Kentucky) Favorite newspaper that while on his deathbed "in a faraway western state" that William confessed to having killed Harvey King. It is here that this story begins to leave the realm of history and ventures into folklore. It is consistent with a belief that if Abraham Owens did indeed know who killed Harvey King but didn't tell, it was probably done by a member of his family. But there is no factual basis to support the story of a deathbed confession in a western state or elsewhere.

A more credible source for who killed Harvey King if Abraham Owens didn't do it comes from Richard H. Collins's "Annals of Kentucky" in which it is detailed that a man named Evans, who was about to be lynched in Kansas, confessed to having murdered a man in Kentucky for which two other men had been hanged. If true, this man would undoubtedly be John Evans. However, like the William Owens Jr. story above, there is no further factual basis to back up this report.

Captain William King's faults were his own, although at times they may have seemed to have come from fate. King chose to rob a train five miles north of his hometown of Franklin, Kentucky. Although the robbers' faces were blackened, it should have occurred to the robbers that they could be recognized by people on the train from Franklin or at least their voices might be recognized. King's idea to derail the train on a forty-foot embankment literally put in motion the burning stove on the express car and set the car ablaze, taking with it the $25,000 that was the primary reason for his plunder. He told his own brother-in-law W. M. Reeder that he would be killed if he told what he knew about the robbery. He told Riley Towe, after Towe had relayed his knowledge about the robbers, that he had a "jar of money" twenty-five miles away that he wanted Towe to accompany him to retrieve. John Evans testified that King offered him $10 to kill Towe on the Saturday night before Harvey King was killed. And King loaned a pistol to Abraham Owens that was used by someone to kill Harvey King, whether that had been King's intention or not.

Did Captain William P. King lie to God on the gallows when he said he didn't kill his brother? It would bring the end of this story back to the beginning of the world when God was told a lie about fratricide East of Eden.

Perhaps it's best to end, instead, on those same gallows with a prayer that was delivered that day:

O God! Solemn is the occasion that has brought us together here today. We pray Thee to draw the thoughts and affections of this large assembly toward Thee, and may we be enabled to concentrate our minds upon Thee, the true source of all our happiness and all our joys. O God! Draw very near these poor young men who must soon be ushered into Thy presence. Thou didst save a persecuting Saul; Thou didst save a thief on the cross. Oh, come and save these poor unfortunate men and give them supporting grace in this their hour of greatest need. We thank Thee that we feel Thou art here; but oh, thyself reveal, and may these prisoners, now to be executed, feel that they have an evidence of their acceptance with God, and may their souls be wafted by heavenly breezes to Abraham's bosom. We beseech Thee, our Heavenly Father, to sustain the father and mothers of these unfortunate men. O how we feel, how much we sympathize with their affectionate mothers. We pray Thee to give them grace to bear this sad affliction. We would not forget, O God, the young and tender wife. May she, O may she lean upon Christ for support and be privileged at last to meet her husband in heaven. We lift our hearts to Thee in behalf of all their relatives and this vast assembly here today. May all of us feel that we too must die soon and give an account for all the deeds done in the body. We pray Thee, one more time, to sustain these poor men and give them grace for their last hour and finally bring them to heaven, for Christ's sake. Amen.

BIBLIOGRAPHY

Manuscript:
"Commonwealth of Kentucky v. William P. King, et al. (SC 1744)" (2008). Manuscripts & Folklife Archives, Western Kentucky University, *MSS Finding Aids*. Paper 642. https://digitalcommons.wku.edu/dlsc_mss_fin_aid/642

Books:
Ditto, John J., Jr. *Louisville & Nashville Railroad Robbers; or, The life of King and Owens: Being a complete account of the Louisville and Nashville train robbery; the Organization, Capture and Trial, Together with the Sentence of King and Owens to be Hung; Their Respite, or Commutation of Sentence and Execution.* Printed by Author, 1867.

Civil War-Era Newspapers:
"The Robbery of the Louisville Train." *(Nashville TN) Daily Press and Times,* November 10, 1866.
"The Guerrilla Outrage on the Nashville Railroad." *Louisville (KY) Daily Courier,* November 10, 1866, page 4.
"The Railroad Marauders." *Louisville (KY) Daily Courier,* November 15, 1866, page 3.
Chicago Tribune, Saturday, November 17, 1866, page 1.
"Capture of John Evans in a Cave in Simpson County—Final Chapter in the Romance of the Road." *Louisville (KY) Daily Courier,* Nov. 19, 1866, page 3.
"$10,000 Reward!" *Louisville (KY) Daily Courier,* November 20, 1866, page 2.
"Judge George C. Rogers." *Louisville (KY) Daily Courier,* December 15, 1866. page 1.

"The Nashville Train Robbers." *Louisville (KY) Daily Courier*, December 14, 1866, page 2.

"The Railroad Robbers." *Louisville (KY) Daily Courier*, January 16, 1867, page 1.

"Trial of the Railroad Robbers." *Louisville (KY) Daily Courier*, January 21, 1867, page 2.

"The Railway Robbers." *Louisville (KY) Daily Courier*, January 22, 1867, page 2.

"The Railway Robbers." *Louisville (KY) Daily Courier*, January 25, 1867, page 4.

"The Train Robbers and Murderers." Louisville *(KY) Daily* Courier, January 26, 1867, page 1.

"The Convicted Railroad Robbers." Louisville *(KY) Daily* Courier, February 6, 1867, page 3.

"The Railroad Robbers—A Visit to the Prison." Louisville (KY) Daily Courier, June 27, 1867, page 1.

"The Railroad Marauders." *Nashville (TN) Union and American*, June 29, 1867, page 3.

"The Gallows." *New York Herald*, June 29, 1867, page 8.

"Execution of William P. King and Abram Owens at Franklin, Ky." *Sacramento Daily Union*, July 27, 1867.

"The Execution at Franklin." Louisville *(KY) Daily* Courier, July 1, 1867, page 2.

"From Simpson County." Louisville *(KY) Daily* Courier, July 1, 1867.

Internet Sources:
"Ellis Harper." Tennessee Department of Tourist Development. https://www.tnvacation.com/civil-war/person/2057/ellis-harper/

Government Publications:
Assignment of Bankrupt's Effects. District Court of the United States, District of Kentucky. Petition of Peter Finn, 1868.

U.S. Bureau of the Census. "Eighth Census of the United States, 1860: Population." Washington, DC. Government Printing Office, 1864.

U.S. Bureau of the Census. "Ninth Census of the United States, 1870: Population." Washington, DC. Government Printing Office.

U.S. Bureau of the Census. "Tenth Census of the United States, 1880: Population." Washington, DC. Government Printing Office.

U.S. Bureau of the Census. "Fourteenth Census of the United States, 1920: Population." Washington, DC. Government Printing Office.

County Historical Documents:

Logan County, Kentucky Archives. Logan County Circuit Court, November Term, 1867.

Simpson County, Kentucky Archives. Simpson County Circuit Court, September Term, 1867.

Simpson County, Kentucky Archives. Simpson County Circuit Court, December Term, 1867.

Simpson County, Kentucky Archives. Simpson County Circuit Court, March Term, 1868.

Simpson County, Kentucky Archives. Simpson County Circuit Court, September Term, 1868.

Simpson County, Kentucky Archives. Simpson County Circuit Court, March Term, 1869.

ABOUT THE AUTHOR

Russ Witcher grew up in Red Boiling Springs, Tennessee, just south of the Kentucky border. He graduated in 1980 with a journalism degree from Western Kentucky University in Bowling Green. He continued his studies at the University of Tennessee-Knoxville, graduating with a master's degree in communication in 1985.

Russ began his teaching career that year as a journalism instructor at Enterprise State Junior College in Enterprise, Alabama. Returning home to Tennessee in 1989, he began teaching journalism at Tennessee Tech University in Cookeville, Tennessee. While continuing to teach at Tennessee Tech, he continued his graduate studies part-time in 1992 by commuting to the University of Tennessee-Knoxville and obtained his doctoral degree in communication in 2000.

He is currently a full professor of communication at Tennessee Tech and has published four books previously, all pertaining to the Vietnam War and Watergate era.

He lives in Cookeville with his wife, Tera, and teenaged son, Jackson.

ABOUT THE PUBLISHER

The Sager Group was founded in 1984. In 2012 it was chartered as a multimedia content brand, with the intent of empowering those who create art—an umbrella beneath which makers can pursue, and profit from, their craft directly, without gatekeepers. TSG publishes books; ministers to artists and provides modest grants; and produces documentary, feature, and commercial films. By harnessing the means of production, The Sager Group helps artists help themselves. For more information, please see TheSagerGroup.net.

MORE BOOKS FROM THE SAGER GROUP

The Swamp: Deceit and Corruption in the CIA
An Elizabeth Petrov Thriller (Book 1)
by Jeff Grant

Chains of Nobility: Brotherhood of the Mamluks (Book 1-3)
by Brad Graft

Meeting Mozart:
A Novel Drawn from the Secret Diaries of Lorenzo Da Ponte
by Howard Jay Smith

Death Came Swiftly: A Novel About the Tay Bridge Disaster of 1879
by Bill Abrams

A Boy and His Dog in Hell: And Other Stories
by Mike Sager

The Deadliest Man Alive: Count Dante, The Mob
and the War for American Martial Arts
by Benji Feldheim

Lifeboat No. 8: Surviving the Titanic
by Elizabeth Kaye

The Pope of Pot:
And Other True Stories of Marijuana and Related High Jinks
by Mike Sager

See our entire library at TheSagerGroup.net